HOW TO PROFIT FROM GOOGLE ADSENSE

ANTHONY EKANEM

Contents

Preface

For many years now, Google AdSense has dominated fora, discussions, and newsletters all over the Internet and beyond. Already, there are stories of great riches to be made and millions of Dollars made by people who are just working from home. Google AdSense has dominated the internet marketing business and is now considered by many the easiest way to make money on the internet.

The key to success with AdSense is the placing of ads on pages that are receiving high traffic for high demand keywords. The higher the advertiser's cost-per-click, the more money you will receive per click from your website. It does not pay to target low cost-per-click keywords and place them on pages that do not receive hits.

With the vast number of people going online and clicking links every day, it is not surprising why Google AdSense has become an instant cash. For some who are just new to this market, it would be a blow to their pride knowing that their homepage is buried somewhere in the little ads promoting other people's services. But then, when they get the idea that they are earning more money that way, all doubts and scepticism are laid to rest.

There are two significant, and intelligent, factors that some successful webmaster and publishers are learning to blend to make money easier using AdSense.

1. **Targeting high traffic pages on your website.** If you check on your logs, you will discover that many of your visitors are taking advantage of the free affiliate marketing resources and eBooks that you are offering on your site. In simple words, your ads are working

effectively and are generating more clicks. It also means more money for you.

2. **Placing AdSense links on pages that are producing little no profit.**By placing AdSense on free resources pages, you will reduce the number of potential customers being lost to other websites. This is tricky, yet effective.

When I learned to work effectively, these two factors are a good source of producing a minimal amount of revenue from a high traffic page. A lot of people are using this tactic to make some extra cash with AdSense. This is also especially rewarding to informational websites that focus their efforts on delivering powerful affiliate links free content to their visitors. Now they can make money from their services.

With the different techniques that people are now using to make money via their AdSense, it is not surprising that Google is doing everything to update their AdSense to maintain their good image.

With all the people spending more time in their AdSense now and still more getting into this line of marketing, there is no doubt about the many new improvements yet to be made. Imagine the smiles on the faces of the webmasters and publishers all around the world if ever they sign up for sub-affiliates and double or even triple the amount that they are already earning.

The very handy money-making feature that is available with AdSense is the ability to filter out URLs. This gives webmasters the option to block low value offers from their pages and competitors to their websites. This is about taking those that are advantageous and removing the ones that seem "useless".

With Google AdSense, the possibilities are limitless. Yet there is also the possibility of someone taking advantage of the easy money process that this internet marketing is giving. If you think about it, these negative aspects may force Google to break down and thrash AdSense in the process.

If that occurs, people will have to go back to the old ways of internet marketing that do not make as much money online and as easily as AdSense. For now, however, Google AdSense is here to stay. As long as people are wanting to earn some easy cash online just using their talents, the future ahead is looking good. Besides, with all the strict guidelines that Google is enforcing over AdSense, it will take a while for the AdSense privileges to be spammed and even terminated.

CHAPTER ONE

Why AdSense Is Important

To know why AdSense is essential for your content sites is to know first how this works. The concept is straightforward if you think about it. The publisher or the webmaster inserts a java script into a particular website. Each time the page is accessed, the JavaScript will pull advertisements from the AdSense program.

The ads that are targeted should therefore be related to the content that is contained on the web page serving the ad. If a website visitor clicks on an advertisement, the webmaster serving the advertisement earns a portion of the money that the advertiser pays the search engine for the click.

The search engine handles all the tracking and payments, providing an easy way for webmasters to display contents and targeted advertisements without having to solicit advertisers, collect funds, and monitor clicks and statistics which are time-consuming tasks.

It appears there is never a shortage of advertisers in the programme from which the search engine pulls the AdSense ads. Additionally, website owners are less concerned about the lack of information search engines are providing and are more focused on making money from the search engines.

The first reason AdSense is essential for content sites is that it already has come a long way in understanding the needs of publishers and webmasters. Together with its endless progression is the arrival of a more advanced system that allows full advert customisation. Webmasters are given a chance to choose from many different types of text ad formats to complement their website better and fit their webpage layout.

The different formatting affords the site owners the possibility of getting more clicks from visitors who may or may not be aware of what they are clicking on. It can as well appeal to the website visitors, thereby making them take the next step of looking up what it is about. This way, those behind the AdSense ad will get their contents read and make money in the process.

The second reason is the ability of the AdSense publishers to track not only how their sites are progressing but also the earnings based on the webmaster-defined channels. The recent improvements in the search engines give webmasters the capability to monitor how their ads are performing using customizable reports that can detail page impressions, clicks and clickthrough rates.

Publishers can track specific ad formats, colours, and pages within their website. They can also easily spot trends. With the real-time reporting at hand, the effectiveness of the changes made will be assessed quickly. There is time to sort out the contents that people are making the highest number of clicks on. The ever-changing demands would be met while generating cash for the webmasters and publishers.

The more flexible tools are also allowing webmasters to group web pages by URL, domain, ad type or category, which will provide them with some accurate insight on which pages, ads and domains are performing best.

The last and final reason is that advertisers have realised the benefits associated with having their ads served on targeted websites, thus increasing the possibility that a prospective web surfer will have an interest in their product and services; all because of the content and its constant maintenance.

As opposed to those who are not using AdSense in their sites, they are given the option of having other people do their content for them, giving them the benefit of having successful and money-generating web sites.

AdSense is about targeted contents; the more targeted your contents are, the more targeted the search engines' adverts will be. There are some webmasters and publishers who are focused more on their site contents and how best to maintain them rather than the cash that the ads will generate for them. This is where the effectiveness is at its best.

There was a time when people were not aware of the money to be made from advertisements. The cash generated only came into existence when the webmasters and publishers realised how they could make AdSense be that generator. In those days, the contents were the most critical factors that were taken quite seriously. It still is. With the allure of money, of course.

CHAPTER TWO

How to Make Money with AdSense

AdSense is deemed one of the most powerful tools in a website publisher's collection. It enables the publisher to monetise their website easily. If used properly, it can generate a substantial and healthy income for them. However, if you are not using them right and just maximizing the income you squeeze from it, you are leaving a lot of money on the table.

How you can start earning money with AdSense can be done easily and quickly. You will be amazed at the results you will be getting in such a short period. Start by writing quality keyword-rich contents and publish them on your website.

There are three steps to put into mind before you begin writing your ads and having an effective AdSense.

Keyword search. Find some popular subjects, keywords, or phrase. Select the ones that you think has more visitors clicking through.

Writing articles. Start writing original contents with keywords from the topics that you have achieved in your search. Take note that search engines are interested in the quality of the articles and what you write should keep up with their demands.

Quality content site. Build a quality content site incorporated with AdSense ads that are targeting the subject and keywords of your articles and websites. This is where all you have done at first will go to, and this is also where they will prove their value to you.

The positioning of your adverts should be done with care. Try to position your ads where your website visitors are most likely to click on them. According to research, the one place that surfers look first when they visit a particular site is the top left. The reason behind this is not known. Perhaps, it is because the most useful search engine results are at the top of other website ranking. So, visitors tend to be looking in that same place when surfing through other websites.

Some of those who are just starting at this business may think they are doing well already and thinking that their clickthrough rates and CPM figures are healthy. However, there are more techniques you can use to generate more clicks and double your earnings. By knowing these techniques and taking advantage of them, you will realise that you will be getting better results.

Finally, AdSense has some excellent tracking statistics that allows webmasters and publishers to track their results across several sites on a site by site, page by page, or any other basis you wanted. You should be aware of this capability and take advantage of it because it is one powerful tool that can help you find out which ads are performing well. This way, you can fine-tune your AdSense ads and focus more on the ones being visited the most rather than those who are being ignored.

Another thing you should know. Banners and skyscrapers are dead. Ask the experts. So better forget about banners and skyscrapers. Surfers universally ignore these kinds of ad formats. The reason is that they are recognised as advertising and advertising are rarely of any interest; that is why people usually ignore them.

To start making money with AdSense, you should have a definite focus on what you wanted to achieve and the way you will go about achieving them. As with other types of business ventures, time is of the essence, coupled with patience.

Do not ignore your website and your AdSense after you have finished implementing them. Create some time adjusting the AdSense ads on your sites to quickly trigger your AdSense income. Give it a try, and you would not regret having gotten into AdSense in the first place.

CHAPTER THREE

How to Improve Your AdSense Earnings

If webmasters want to monetize their websites, the great way to do it is through AdSense. There are lots of webmasters struggling hard to earn some good money a day through their sites. But then some of the "geniuses" of them are enjoying hundreds of Dollars a day from AdSense ads on their websites. What makes these publishers different is that they think outside the box.

Those who have been there and have made it have some useful tips to help the ones who would want to venture into this field. Some of the tips have boosted a lot of earnings and is continuously doing so.

Here are some proven ways on how best to improve your AdSense earnings.

1. **Concentrating on one format of the AdSense ad**. The one format that works well for the majority is the Large Rectangle (336X280). This same format has the tendency to result in higher CTR, or the clickthrough rates. Why select this format out of the various you can use? Because the ads will look like standard web links, and people, being used to clicking on them, click these types of links. They might or might not know they are clicking on your

AdSense, but if there are clicks, then it will all be for your benefit.

2. **Create a custom palette for your ads.** Choose a colour that blends well with the background of your website. If your website has a white background, try to use white as the colour of your ad border and background. The idea of patterning the colours is to make the AdSense look like it is part of the webpages. This will cause more clicks from people who visit your site.

3. **Put your AdSense at the top of your website pages.** Do not hide your AdSense. Put them where people can quickly see them, and you will be surprised at the difference AdSense locations can make when you see your earnings.

4. **Maintain links to relevant websites.** If you think some websites are better than others, put your ads there and manage them. If there is already lots of AdSense, put into that certain site, put yours on top of all of them. That way, the visitor will see your ads first upon landing on that site.

5. **Automate the insertion of your AdSense code into your webpages using SSI (or server-side included).**Ask your web administrator whether your server supports SSI. How do you do it? Just save your AdSense code in a text file, save it as "adsense text", and upload it to the root directory of the webserver. Then using the SSI, call the code on the other pages. This tip is a time-saver, especially for those who are using automatic page generators to generate pages on their website.

These are some of the tips that have worked well for some who want to generate hundreds and even thousands on their websites. It is important to know though that ads are displayed because it fits the interest of the people viewing them. So, focusing on a specific topic should be your primary purpose because the displays will be mainly targeted on a topic that persons will be viewing already.

Note also that there are many other AdSense sharing the same topic as you. It is best to make a good ad that will be a bit different and unique. Every clickthrough that visitors make is a point for you, so make every click count by making your AdSense something that people will click on.

Suggestions given by those who have boosted their earnings are mere guidelines they are sharing with others. If they have worked wonders for some, maybe it can work wonders for you as well. Try them out and see the result it will bring. If others have done it, there is nothing wrong trying it out for yourself.

CHAPTER FOUR

Monetizing Your Website with AdSense

Many have now realised that good money can be made from this source of revenue. Try multiplying those clicks for every page on your website, and you will get a summation of earnings comparable to a monthly residual income with the little effort you have put in.

Google AdSense is a fast and easy way for website publishers of all sizes to display relevant and text-based Google ads on their website's content pages and earn money in the process. The ads shown are related to what your users are looking for on your site. This is the main reason why you both can monetize and enhance your content pages using AdSense.

How much you will be earning will depend on how much the advertisers are willing to pay. It will depend also on the keywords required. If the keywords chosen by the advertisers are in high demand, you could receive more money per click. On the other hand, low demand keywords will earn you just a few cents per click.

So, how can you start making money from your blog or website using Google AdSense?

1. Sign up for an AdSense account. This will take only a few minutes of your time.

2. When the site is accepted, you will be receiving a clip code to include in your web pages. You can insert this code on as many pages or web sites that you want. The AdSense will start appearing immediately after.

3. You will be earning a few cents or some dollars per click when someone starts clicking on the AdSense displayed on any of your web pages. Trying to earn false revenues by repetitively clicking on your ads is a no-no. This will result in a penalty or the possibility of your site being eliminated. The money you have already earned may be lost because of this.

4. View your statistics. You can check your AdSense earnings anytime by logging into your account.

Once your account is up and running working, you may want to pattern it to the various websites that are earning more money than yours. It is important to note that factors are affecting how your website will perform and the amount of money it will give you.

It is a common practice that when a site is earning money, the tendency is for the owner to want to make more out of what they are getting already. It takes some trial and error to attain what you want for your AdSense contents.

HOW TO INCREASE YOUR ADSENSE EARNINGS

1. **Choose one topic per page.**It is best to write content for your page with just a few targeted phrases. The search engine will then serve more relevant ads, which will then result in higher click-throughs.

2. **Using white space around your ad.**This can make your ad stand out from the rest of your page so visitors can spot them easily. There are also choices of colours you can use, provided by search engines, which can complement

the colours of your ad with the webpage colour.

3. **Test your Ad placement.**It is advisable to use the vertical format that runs down the side of the webpage to get more positive results. You can also try the horizontal and vertical formats for a certain period to see which one will give you better results.

4. **More Content-based Pages.**Expand the theme of your website by creating pages that focus more on your keyword phrases. This will enhance the pages for the search engines. It can not only attract more traffic but also make them more relevant for the AdSense to be displayed.

5. **Site Build It.**This is a perfect tool to use to generate lots of AdSense revenues. Site Build It has all the tools needed to quickly achieve a keyword-rich website that can rank high in the search engines. It will also produce a flow of highly targeted traffic to your website.

Most webmasters know that AdSense generates a sizeable source of additional advertising income. That is the reason most of them use it to go after high-paying keywords. They have the list that tells what the keywords are, and they have various methods of identifying them. And yet, after putting up these supposed-to-be high paying keywords into their pages, the money they expected to come rolling in is not coming in.

What is it that they are doing wrong?

Having webpages with the right keywords is one thing. But driving visitors to those webpages is another thing entirely, and often the factor that is lacking. The thing is, to get visitors to your high paying keyword pages, you need to optimize your site navigation.

Stop for a while and think about how your website visitors interact with your website. After a visitor has landed on a specific page, they tend to click on another page that sounds interesting. They get there because of the other links that appear on a page that they initially landed on. This is site navigation. It is all about enabling visitors to move about your site; and one way of maximizing your AdSense earnings.

A conventional website has menu links on each page. The wording on these links is what grabs a visitor's attention and gets them to click on one of the links that will take them to another page of that website. Links that have "free' or "download" are often good attention-grabbers.

This logic can also be used to drive traffic to your high-paying webpages. Some websites are getting a lot of traffic from search engines but have low earnings. The trick is to try and use come cleverly labelled links to get the visitors off that pages and navigate them to the higher-earning ones. This is one great way of turning real cheap clicks to real dollars.

Before you begin testing if this same style will work for you and your website, you need to have two things: something to track and compare and some high earning pages you want to funnel your site traffic to. An option is to select a few of your frequently visited pages. This is ensuring fast result to come by.

Now, what you should do next is to think of ways to get visitors viewing a particular page on your website to click on the links that will take them to your high-earning pages. Come up with a catchy description for that link. Think of something that people do not get to see every day. That will spark their interest enough to want to see what that was all about.

You may also use graphics to grab the attention of your readers. There is no limitation to what you can do to make your link noticeable. If you care about the success of your blog or website, you will do whatever it takes to achieve that goal. Just be creative. As far as AdSense advertisers are concerned, there is no written or unwritten law to follow concerning what they write. Just as long as you do not overstep the guidelines of the search engines, then go for it.

Also remember that location is very important. Once the perfect attention-grabbing description has been achieved, you have to identify the ideal spot on your page to position that descriptive link to your high paying page.

Nothing is wrong with visiting other blogs or websites to see how they are maximizing their site navigation. "Hot pages" or "Most read" lists are widespread and overly used already. Get to know those that many websites are already using and do not try to imitate them.

An alternative way of doing it is to use different texts on different pages. That way, you will see the ones that work and what does not. Try to mix things around also. Put links on top and sometimes on the bottom too. This is how you go about testing which ones get more clicks and which ones are being ignored. Let the testing begin. Testing and tracking until you find the site navigation style that works best for your site.

CHAPTER FIVE

Increase Your AdSense Earnings

AdSense is making a significant impact on the affiliate marketing industry nowadays. Because of this, weak affiliate merchants tend to die faster than ever, and ad networks will be going to lose their customers quickly. If you are losing rather than winning in the affiliate programme you are currently into, maybe it is about time to consider going into the AdSense marketing and start earning some real cash.

Google is providing well-written and highly relevant ads that can closely match the content on your webpages. You do not have to look for them yourself as the search engine will be doing the search for you from other people's sources. You do not have to spend time choosing a different kind of ads for different pages. And there are no codes to mess around for various affiliate programmes.

You will be able to concentrate on providing good and quality content, as the search engines will be the ones finding the best ads in which to put your pages on. You will still be allowed to add AdSense ads even if you already have affiliate links on your blog or website. It is forbidden, however, to mimic the look and feel of the Google ads for your affiliate links.

You can filter up to 200 URLs. That gives you an opportunity to block advertising for the websites that do not meet your standards. You can also block competitors, though it is inevitable that AdSense may be competing for space on websites that other revenues are sharing.

Proprietors of small websites or blogs can plug a code into their websites and instantly have relevant text ads that appeal to their visitors appear instantly into their pages. If you own different blogs or websites, you only need to apply once. It makes up for having to apply to many affiliate programmes.

The payment rates can vary significantly. The payment you will receive per click will depend on how much advertisers pay per click to advertise with the use of Google AdWords. Advertisers can pay as little as 5 cents and as high as $10 to $12, sometimes even more than that. You are earning a share of the money generated.

If your results are stagnant, it can help if you build simple and uncluttered webpages so that the advertising can catch the visitor's attention more. It sometimes pays to do things differently from the usual things other people are doing. It is also a refreshing sight for your visitor once they see something different for a change.

Publishers also have the option of choosing to have their ads displayed only on a particular site or sites. It is also allowed to have them displayed on an extensive network of sites. The choice depends on what you think will work best for you.

To know whether some AdSense ads you see on the search engines have your webpages, try to find webpages that have similar contents as yours and look up their AdSense ads.

It is important to note that you cannot choose specific topics only. If you try this, search engines will not place AdSense advertising on your website, and you will be missing out on opportunities to earn money. It is prudent to look at other people's information and tailor your AdSense appropriately. Just think about it as doing yourself a favour by not having to work too hard to know what content to have.

With all the information that people need in your hands already, all you have to do is turn them as your profits. It all boils down to a gain and gain situation both for the content site owners and the webmasters or publishers. Make other people's matter your own and start earning some extra cash.

CHAPTER SIX

How to Avoid Account Termination

Google, being the leader in search engines, places high importance on the quality and relevance of its search engines. To keep the shareholders and users of its engines happy, the quality of the returned results is given extreme importance. For this reason, doing the wrong things with AdSense and other forms of advertisements, whether intentionally or otherwise, will result in a severe penalty. It can get you banned or even have your account terminated.

Therefore, for those who are thinking of making money from AdSense, do not only think of the strategies you will be using to earn more money. Consider some things first before you get involved.

Hidden texts. Filling your advertisement page with texts too small to read, has the same colour as the background and using CSS for the sole purpose of loading them with rich keywords content and a copy will earn you a penalty award that is given to those who are hiding links.

Page cloaking. There is a common practice of using the browser or bot sniffers to serve the bots of a different page other than the page your visitors will see. Loading a webpage with a bot that a human user will never see is not advisable. This is tricking them to click on something that you want, but they may not want to go to.

Multiple submissions. Submitting multiple copies of your domain or pages is another thing to avoid. For instance, trying to submit a URL of an AdSense as two separate URLs can lead to account termination. This is a reason to avoid auto-submitters for those who are receiving submissions.

Link farms. Be careful of what are you linking your AdSense to. Search engines know that you cannot control your inbound links. But you can control what your outbound links. Link farming has always been a rotten apple in the eyes of search engines, especially Google. That is why you must avoid them. Having a link higher than 100 on a single page will classify you as a link farm, so try and not to make them higher than that.

Page rank for sale. If you have been online for quite some time, you will notice that some sites are selling their PR links or trading them with other websites. If you do this, expect a ban anytime from Google. It is fine to sell ads or gain the link but doing it on direct advertisement of your page rank is not acceptable to the search engines.

Doorways. This is like cloaking pages. The common practice of a page loaded with keyword ads aimed at redirecting visitors to another page is a big issue with search engines. Many SEO firms are offering this kind of services. Now that you know what they are trying to avoid them at all costs.

Multiple domains have the same content. In case you are not aware of it, search engines look at domains IP's, registry dates and many others. Having multiple domains having the same content is not something you can hide from them. The same goes with content multiplied many times on separate pages, sub-domains and forwarding multiple domains to the same content.

Many of the techniques described above apply to most search engines and Google alone. By having a mindset that you are building your AdSense together with your pages for the human users and not for bots, you can be assured of the great things for your ads and website or blog.